# Noah's Story

Written by Grace Kim
Edited and illustrated by Noah Hylkema

Copyright © 2018 Grace Kim.

Illustrations © Noah Hylkema.

All rights reserved. No part of this book may be used or reproduced by any means, graphic, electronic, or mechanical, including photocopying, recording, taping or by any information storage retrieval system without the written permission of the copyright owner except in the case of brief quotations embodied in critical articles and reviews.

Because of the dynamic nature of the Internet, any web addresses or links contained in this book may have changed since publication and may no longer be valid.

The views expressed in this work are solely those of the authors and do not necessarily reflect the views of the publisher and the publisher hereby disclaims any responsibility for them.

National Library of Australia
Cataloguing-in-Publication data:
Noah's Story
ISBN: 978-0-6484525-5-3 (hc)
ISBN: 978-0-6484525-4-6 (sc)
ISBN: 978-0-6484525-3-9 (e)
Juvenille non-fiction, general.

Publisher details: Karen Mc Dermott
www.karenmcdermott.com.au

Team Noah -  Jane, Josey, Bronwyn
Our family - Teije, Tom,
Grandparents in Australia and Holland
and
the teachers at Korowal and Hazelbrook Public School

Hi, my name is Noah. I am seven years old.

I live with my mum, dad, and brother Tommy, my two goldfish and a cat named Sophie.

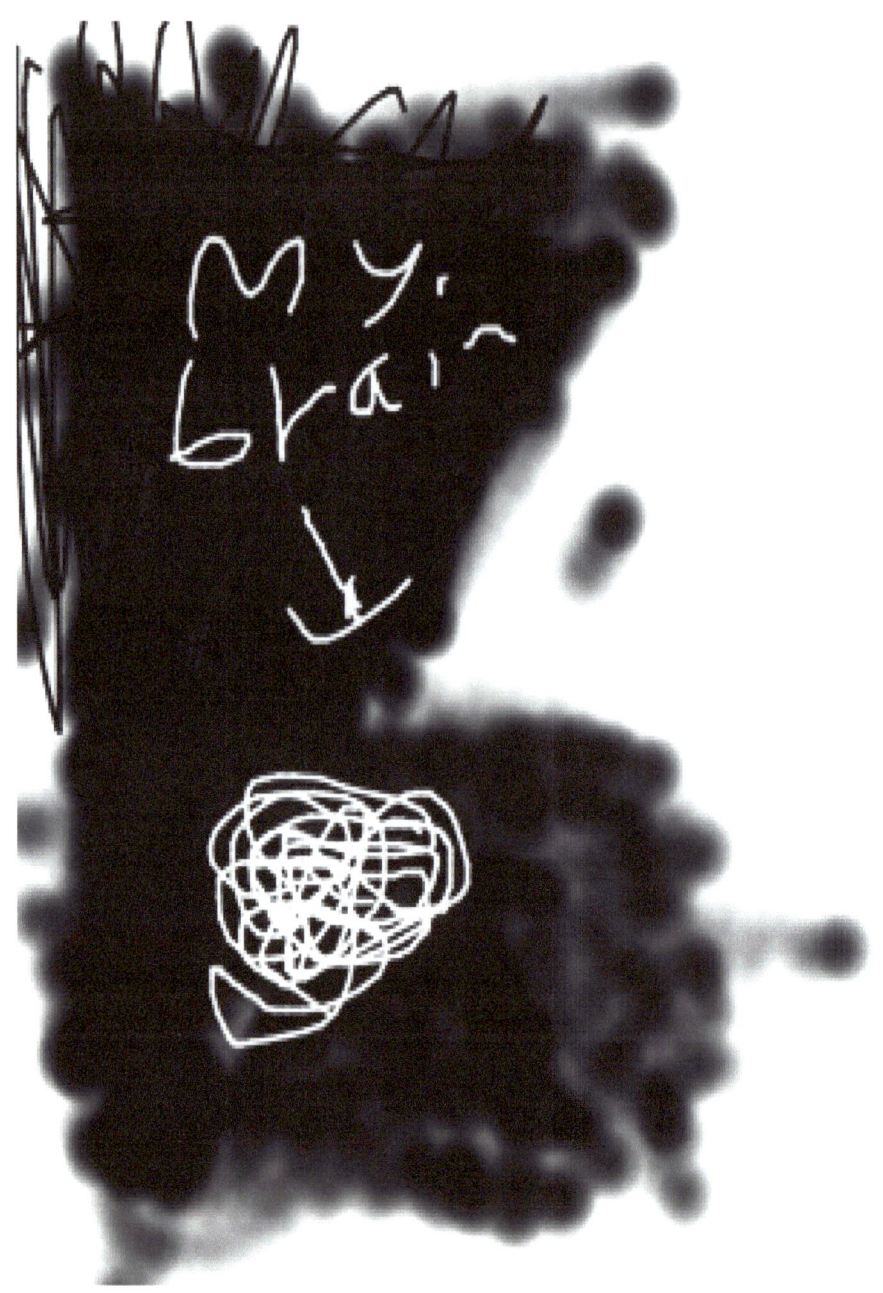

I have high functioning Autism, also known as Asperger's Syndrome.

This means my brain works a little differently to yours.

I can get very confused about things that may be simple to you, but things that might be difficult for you may be simple to me!

Situations involving lots of people, such as school, playground and parties, are very confusing to me.

My brain finds it very hard to know what is the right 'rule' to get along with people.

It's a bit like if you are visiting a foreign country and you are not sure of their culture and customs.

Sometimes I find looking at people's eyes too distracting, which means I can't focus on the words, so I tend to look away.

But people think I'm not listening to them, even though I am actually listening better this way.

So I'm learning to try to remember to look at their eyes, but please understand if I forget.

Certain smells that other people may not notice, might be so strong for me that I can't focus on anything else but trying to block it.

When I am busy doing this, I may not hear you calling my name.

Banging, loud noises, like cheering, hurt my ears and make me stressed.

I may try to escape the noise.

My mind sometimes gets so stuck on a word, a game or a musical beat that I might not hear you greeting me.

I feel sad and lonely when nobody plays with me.

I want to join in at the playground but am not sure how, so I may sometimes just push or say something shocking to get your attention.

I don't really mean to hurt you. I'm learning that this is not a good way to make friends. Maybe you can remind me.

I like to share my interests, funny jokes and stories with you, but I may be going on and on about it in a loud voice.

I'm learning that this can be uncomfortable. Maybe you can remind me to speak softer, or to pause, so that you can share too.

When it all gets too much, I need to find a quiet spot to be by myself.

I feel sadness, anger, happiness, just like anyone else. I may just show them differently.

I am working hard to learn these social rules. I have a wonderful team of teachers, professionals and parents helping me.

Sometimes I will make mistakes, but I know that means I'm trying and learning.

I'm glad I have an Asperger's brain. My brain can process information faster than a bullet, and can remember so many interesting facts.

I don't forget information easily, especially if it's on a topic I'm interested in!

I can also read and write numerous stories for hours and hours, my mind is always full of wonderful stories.

Many famous people like Albert Einstein, Isaac Newton, Sir Anthony Hopkins and Stanley Kubrick all had Asperger's brain too.

I hope you understand me a little better now.

I'm still learning, just like you.

# Why Grace Kim wrote Noah's Story

In 2016, my son Noah was seven years old when he was given a diagnosis of High Functioning Autism (Asperger's syndrome) after a long period of challenging experiences at school.

Being the person I am, I immediately started to read all the books, attending workshops and seminars regarding Autism, to understand this condition, and also to find a way to disclose this information to Noah, and to his classmates.

After reading a mountain of books, I still couldn't find a book that resonated with us personally. So one desperate night, I decided to write a story from Noah's perspective to help him, his friends and teachers understand him and his diagnosis. I showed it to Noah to check with him if I represented his feelings correctly (thankfully, yes!) and asked if he would like to do some drawings for it, to take it to the school the next day. This ended up being a wonderful way to introduce the subject and for him to be fully involved and in control of his 'coming out'.

It was never intended as 'I'm going to write a book', it was just a mother's earnest attempt to help others understand her son. I hope this will give you the courage to tell your own story.

## About the illustrator
# Noah Hylkema

Noah is nine years old and has been writing and illustrating stories since he was four years old. Noah loves reading, coding, building websites and games, and playing with his brother, Tom.

Noah would like to dedicate this book to his best friend, Dylan, who is always in his corner.

Currently, Noah is a student at Hazelbrook Public School in the Blue Mountains.

# About the author
# Grace Kim

As a Winston Churchill Fellow, concert pianist, artistic director, music educator, wife and mother, Grace enjoys her diverse roles in her professional and personal life. Grace has performed as concert soloist with major symphony orchestras of Australasia, Belgium, Turkey, Russia and Ukraine. She is a prizewinner of numerous international and national competitions and awards.

A mother of two young children, Grace is a passionate advocate for music education. She is the founding Creative Director of Sensory Concerts to provide quality classical music concerts for families with sensory/special needs, and was selected as a national finalist in the 2018 AusMumpreneur Award in two categories: Making a Difference, and Big Idea Award.

Returning after an international career as a professional pianist and teacher in The Netherlands, she is now based in Sydney and the Blue Mountains. Grace currently teaches at the Rising Stars Program at Sydney Conservatorium of Music, and lives with her husband, two children Noah and Tom, and a cat named Sophie.

www.gracekim.com.au

www.ingramcontent.com/pod-product-compliance
Lightning Source LLC
Chambersburg PA
CBHW042144290426
44110CB00002B/105